THE FIFTH WINDOW

THE FIFTH WINDOW

RUSSELL THORNTON

THISTLEDOWN PRESS

Canada Cataloguing in Publication

The fifth window
Poems.
ISBN 978-1-894345-09-5
I. Title
PS8589.H565 F54 2000 C811'.54 COO-920060-6
PR9199.3.T485 F54 2000

Printed and bound in Canada

Thistledown Press Ltd.
P.O. Box 30105 Westview
Saskatoon, Saskatchewan, S7L 7M6
www.thistledownpress.com

Thistledown Press gratefully acknowledges the financial assistance of the Canada Council for the Arts, SK Arts, and the Government of Canada for its publishing programs.

ACKNOWLEDGEMENTS

A number of the poems in this book have appeared in the following magazines and anthologies:

Arc, *Backwater Review*, *BC Studies*, *Canadian Literature*, *Descant*, *The Fiddlehead*, *The Gaspereau Review*, *Grain*, *The Literary Review of Canada*, *The Malahat Review*, *The New Quarterly*, *Poetry Canada Review*, *TickleAce*, *The Windsor Review*, *Vintage 96* (Quarry Press, 1997), *Foreign Language Poems on Thessaloniki* (Kedros Publishers, Athens, Greece, 1997), and *The Edges of Time* (Seraphim Editions, 1999).

Some of the poems also appeared in *The Accurate Earth*, a limited edition chapbook published by Reference West in 1997.

My thanks to Susan Musgrave for her editorial eye.

NOTES

The poems in section II are all set in Greece. The poems in section III, with the exception of "Morning on Wickaninnish Beach" and "Savary Island Light", are set in North Vancouver.

CONTENTS

I

III

IV

Five windows light the cavern'd man: thro' one he breathes the air;
Thro' one, hears music of the spheres; thro' one, the eternal vine
Flourishes, that he may receive the grapes; thro' one can look
And see small portions of the eternal world that ever groweth;
Thro' one, himself pass out what time he pleases . . .

— William Blake, from *EUROPE*

I

YOUR ANKLET

That chain fringed with metal, beads, and loose bells
you wear around your slender ankle,
it is like a travelling orchestra
arriving out of melting hilltop mist,
its tambourines jingling with your each step,
it is like just-beginning ringing rain,
but you have come here from a dry country
where such anklets are known to have been worn
by women who laboured in feudal fields,
and if one turned aside or wandered off
to open to a man, others would hear
the bells and know.
                                        Now you are back in that
sun-laden, austere, voluptuous land,
but here, I go out into a morning
of mist perfumed with the incense of green trees,
of dew that is moon-breath and moon-metal
the night has left in the grass, abundant
burning, coruscating dew, and the bells,
the innumerable bells of the dew,
are ringing below hearing, violet-edged,
their unseen clappers darkening the air,
and they are the bells in you beneath your skin,
it is as if suddenly you are with me
and announcing it to the world, though only
you and I can hear.
                                        Out in the mist fields
the bells' sound opens paths through the grassblades,
through the vaporous weddings of change and change,
they lead us, they are our own caresses,
and the place where we meet is darkness, secret
darkness hidden in the glare of the sun,
it is the invisible, and there, for
short moments, we are its living adornment.

North Vancouver

LADY HENNA

You have left henna in your hair for the night
as you do at the end of each month,
now the scent has lain down in my bed,

and I have come to think that it is henna
that has coloured the nails of your hands and feet,
and now your menstrual blood

has stained the sheet a vivid, shining red
as if it were warm henna, and its scent is that of the summer sun
in an ancient field of long grass,

the scent rolls subtly from your body
like another body, smoky and invisible.
You wrap the sheet around us like a cloth garment

dyed red, and you take me deeper
into the living fragrance of your body,
with flowing lunar blood you anoint me,

now a henna shrub thrives in my bed,
the scent of the henna is ushering itself
out of its plant roots, the white flower of the henna

is budding along its branches, because you have woven us
in a scarlet sheet, the travelling visiting henna leaves and flowers
are appearing in our veins, which are those of another body,

so we inhale and exhale the air of a circling scent,
the scent releases itself from the waves of your hair,
now we wake inside each other again and again.

THE KOHL OF MY EYES

The black around your eyes
had disappeared, and you were at the mirror
re-applying the make-up you use
made of fine powdered antimony mixed with fragrant oils.

I saw a woman in the room
as against a theatre backdrop of darkness —
the long curtain of her hair swayed and revealed her as she turned
like the hair of a woman in a story
who stood a moment at a balcony window
because of one who longed for her from the dust of the street.
It was not you, it was she who presided over us.
And yet it was you.

You were drawing blackness
along the edges of your eyelids
and brightening your eyes,
and I rose to watch you,
and you turned and faced me, smiling, holding back your hair,
your flesh a white torch-flame.

And I saw how you yourself
are the kohl of my own eyes' outlines,
bringing light into my eyes,
and how she who is always travelling in you, she who reveals
through your flesh and your gestures that you are made of light,
lets your image sing in my eyes.

THE ORCHARD

For in this Period the Poet's work is Done, and all the
Great Events of Time start forth & are conceiv'd in such a Period,
Within a Moment, a Pulsation of the Artery.

— William Blake, *Milton*

Last night, your monthly blood
spotted the sheet like spilled wine.

Drink this, you said to me later, in my dream,
it will give you a poem,

and you offered me wine
from a pitcher in your lap.

And then, in the morning, when you had drawn me into you,
through my skin, I saw an orchard flash against a blackness —

with our bodies we had halved
a single piece of the fruit;

we were sharing it, sharing the entire orchard together;
in an orchard that was red, the red of your womb's blood,

in an orchard-world we were tasting union;
in the moment between two pulse-beats,

the wine had consumed us,
and was itself intoxicated.

We lay winded, indistinguishable,
like identical twins,

our skins brilliant inside and out,
having just come into the flesh,

like human fruit, with its own winepress in it,
like the wine itself, the always desiring wine.

THE BODY OF THE WHISPERING

The summer air's ghostly stillness
is invisibly plundering the tree,
the leaf-flesh so green in its fullness, and so still itself
and yet in motion, like the shape of a woman.

It is whispering, its stillness
is whispering as into the tree's ears;
it has seen its face in the tree's green mirror.

The vivid body of the leaves
will perish, like that of a condemned seer, a woman too knowing —
the bright body of the whispering,
in its longing for the leaves' transience, will gather up the leaves
into the invisible, and so gather up the mirroring woman,
who will now never again wish, suffer, or change.

I see the tree filling with a fire
that is cold, clear, clean as an eye;
I stand here in a dissolution suddenly no longer my own.

The leaves of the beautiful tree
are at the point of disappearing,
are elsewhere melting like ore
into a transparent metal.

THE ACCURATE EARTH

not love, lean and frequent,
but the accurate earth

— Gwendolyn MacEwen, "The Self Assumes"

The sunlight is visible music in the grass —
the notes of the one who so moved the king and queen
of the underworld with his lyre playing and singing
that he was given his beloved back from the dead,
and led her up toward the light of day, but turned to her too soon,
and looked into the face of love and saw a face eaten away;
it is the song he could sing only when he had lost her
a second time, and watched her fade from him forever —
only when he had become too desperate to love.
Somewhere in the grass now is his never to be found skull,
the summer air moving through and through it
and through the silent unperturbed growing green,
the lit blades the only calling and telling of the story —
of how even when she had let go of his hand,
the fire in each of them trying to burn the distance between them
had already changed itself into grass,
the way grass is always becoming grass.
Somewhere the song is heard; somewhere it is not this fire,
though this fire might, to us, be infinite, precise,
and, if it is grass, pure green without limit; somewhere
it is not this love, though this love might, to us, be accurate,
as the earth is, and beyond joy and sorrow, beyond love.

FOUR CRIES

The sound a seagull makes
at exactly four a.m.
is four sharp quick impersonal
perfect cries
of a thing suddenly
terrifyingly alive,
infant-like and old,
a desolate ghost
instantly collecting up
the entire world
in its lament
and opening it like a door,
the always lost thing
that something in us
listens for and knows
apart from us,
a single white petal
of spirit now
here here here here,
a stark brilliant rib
torn out of the invisible,
rushing through the blackness
of the empty street,
all the burning couples
dreaming and turning
together in their sheets.

NIGHT TIDE

In a dream I watched a tide rushing to fullness,
drawing out long shore grass as it wove through sand dunes;
I walked east, the seawater flowing to my side —
beautiful, unearthly, wild, lit, animal touch.
Something like church bells began ringing, sending out
their own sudden tide of rhythmic clapping,
a clear chant across the sky; I walked toward them,
suddenly aware I was no longer what I had been.
I reached a tower, a room with a high ceiling, with stone walls,
sat at an oak desk and began writing quickly
and in a deep calm. Somewhere within the dream dark
I had been ushered into a nearness to one
whose flesh was so subtle, so awake, that outside a window,
in the black sky, a petal broke continually
into cold white flame but was not consumed.
I thought, as a tide swung and flooded to a shore,
so a body moved; as a body, so a soul
in its miracle turnings. Then an old woman
was at the open door. "We're all leaving," she said.
"I know," I told her, looking up. "I'll be ready."
"You won't be able to keep her a secret any more,
will you?" she announced. While I watched her turn and go,
I felt the one she had spoken of showing through my face.

SAPPHO'S MOON

Eros, weaver of tales
— Sappho

A woman who is you and not you
is standing naked by the window,
the burden of her desire on her,
and the anonymous touch
of the moon, its soft dazzle
that is the story of light.
And she is asking that her desire
be woven into the story,
that she be released from her body
through her body, the moon's touch
turn her flesh to metaphor.
It is a night she knows she must wait —
as if she has always waited —
in front of a moon of waiting,
and the light made of distance
that brings the world to the world,
and the light made of her asking
to live in her life, that remains
as her desire grows outward
and twines with sorrow, and remains.
It is the light Sappho saw
and felt journeying through her,
shining now in the flesh of one
who is standing by a window,
who I will not know what to call
when I awake again beside her.
It is the story hidden in the flesh
that will tell us of the light
that shines from every form
in its elsewhere beyond desire,

but here must be woven together,
and her desire weave her a garment
of a subtle, endless cloth
that will wrap itself around her
and become her nakedness,
weaving a garment for the moon.

THE DAUGHTER OF THE WORKER IN GOLD

I say your last name silently to myself —
I toss it into a still pool, and the sudden circle
propagates and widens like expanding gold
until it seems it holds within itself all sound and all light.
Generation after generation,
they must have uttered this name and marvelled
as at an exquisite command, they who knew
they would be lifelong workers in gold —
your father, his father, his father's father —
who would watch gold melt, and pour, and then shine
in circlets, necklaces, rings, bracelets, anklets —
all the array of adornments they made
and showed in the bazaars in their cities and villages.
Their eyes would fill with illumination
as they performed their ecstatic labour, as they imagined you
hidden in the most precious and the softest of metals,
generation after generation,
as they became pure ritual at work benches,
as they felt nature's desire alive in their hands.
They would wait, they would know a bright moment
when they would abandon everything they were
forever to a woman whose flesh was like the sun's,
and who could thread the earth's most intimate secret
like gold embroidery through their twinned loins —
until a he and she found one another, and were found,
whose love would usher you into the world,
and let you leave and travel far from what they knew.
And this is how you came to gild my days,
and your last name tell me of the knowledge it keeps —
of what is within gold and more perfect than gold,
of the lender of light to gold and all metals,
of the key to many doors, and of the unknown one at each door.

And it is as if what lies in it allows the muteness in me
to open now through your last name as I say it,
and allows us to inhabit one another
in an instant in which something steps through us,
and makes us nameless, living gold, pointing the way to gold.

THE MUSK

All day, though you were not here, I could smell you,
your heavy hair falling over me, your naked shoulder;
the first breeze of spring came through the open window
and touched your sweater, releasing your scent from the wool;
I put it to my face and breathed you in.
Then when I sat at the table, wanting to write about you,
I could think only of how once, on a park trail
in the late afternoon, I felt I had been joined by a presence,
and turned and beheld a doe that had been following me;
she stood there in her animal stillness watching me,
recognition reverberating between us like a monastery bell,
and I became strange to myself, and half afraid,
my eyes copying the shining wet blackness of her gaze;
then, as if to tell me she had truly been there,
the forest light grew brighter, and darker edged,
and, deepening its dazzle, revealed its grainy powder
falling as through emanations of suffering and joy,
until it stood, the solid perfume of itself, as a great tree,
and the doe vanished down a bough-lined aisle.
That night, while I held you, you convulsed beautifully in sleep,
your belly undulating, and you cried out,
quickened by some unfathomable intimate touch,
having dreamt the essence of happiness,
and you woke as you came involuntarily, turning to me,
opening astonished eyes, eyes darker now,
without saying anything, asking me to enter you.
And the next day, alone on a suburban street, suddenly
I saw a wild deer for the third time in my life, then two,
going from yard to yard, standing beneath trees, lifting their mouths
to nibble at the brilliant white masses of May blossoms;
together they bounded tawny-haunched toward me,
and as they passed, they seemed to bound through me,
two souls allowed a few instants in the world
in which to know exquisite desperation, to need to know
nothing but one another before they had to leave.

They ran on into the shadows of woods between houses,
leaving the sound of the blossoms floating to grass,
the air's vibration fragrant, a sound I inhaled,
the music of things coming into being and dying;
I saw myself entering you then as entering vision beyond sight,
soft wind ushering me, the breath of the breath,
which would fill my blood, and let it steep me in you,
and bring me to an ecstatic nearness to you,
and there where it had always waited hidden
and where it would now pour out, the musk had grown stronger,
and the scent of longing touched you in the night.

RAIN OF SEEING

You find a lit hidden place in the rain
as after having gone to and fro half your life through a house of mirrors
in which your image looking back at you in a thousand ways
posed a riddle that sought you out, a question
that only you could answer, and, answering, unaware,
you made your life a question, a circling round a woman like a centre,
one who lived with you in the house, and waited to show herself
and open a door and let you go through and walk towards her.
You find you are here as after having gone to and fro and been defeated,
and understood then that what you asked and asked for was her
while all along she knew you, and could see you,
but could only lament that you were absent from her,
and you find you are here as if finally old and blind and lost enough,
and reach your hand out now to a presence you sense,
and it takes your hand, and the rain ushers you into the rain.
And you ask yourself where the house is, and have no answer.
And the rain is such as you have never stood in before,
scattering its drops over you, over everything around you,
and seeming to see through its drops, its innumerable fingertips,
everything lifting to meet them at each touch.
The trees and leaves you see are made of rain,
the grasses, the natural rock you rest on, are made of rain.
And you yourself are now nothing but an infinite rain
that has stopped in you, and has always been falling in you,
and has ushered you here so you may learn a new blindness.
It is as if something is being written by each drop to the other,
but you cannot decipher it before it disappears as it touches you,
as each drop splashes, and is lost in what you know the rain
is conjuring up, in exquisite cups, in bodies turning and turning.
Because you are now blind with rain, you feel rain touching rain,
and rain displaying itself to itself at last.

And you feel a caress that never ends
in this place that gathers you up, and re-names your sorrow,
in this place where you are your own lock and key, and where you will die,
and where you are all the rain seeing, each drop
dispersing you through all the rain's drops, which in turn touch you,
and let you ceaselessly dissolve yourself
as a single drop in a rain of seeing, answerless and joyous.

A WOMAN WASHING

And it came to pass in an eventide, that David arose from off his bed,
and walked upon the roof of the king's house: and from the roof
he saw a woman washing herself; and the woman was very beautiful
to look upon.

— II Samuel 11:

You lean over the sink, and take running water in your hands
and touch it to your face and down your neck.
At the bright bathroom sink, in the morning, you wash yourself,
as if in a place you have never been before,
come out of the night as to a cool stream.
Now you turn and throw your hair down, and bend low,
and run your fingers flowing with water down through it,
wetting and deftly smoothing the thick strands.
The early sun coming through the window,
caressing you along the nape of your neck,
finding its way through the falling folds,
you fix your hair, and fling it all at once
up and back, straighten, and begin again.
You are not the woman who was once watched
by a man who rose from his bed and walked the roof of the king,
and from the roof saw her washing herself
and saw she was beautiful to look upon.
But I want to watch you as if I were a man in a story,
and live in the turnings of the words that flow into you —
into what you feel as you make love,
into the melting light of your night's dream,
into the longing burning at the story's centre.
I want to watch you as on this morning always,
and a part of myself find you, and lose you, and find you
in a moment of exquisite crisis
in which you stand taut-haunched and wash yourself,

tending to your hair without comb or brush,
a slender animal come into the house, a woman
with knowledge of every holy story known until now
in her hands, her every movement washing away
those stories, and telling this new one wordlessly.

THE HEALED ROSE

But first the notion that man has a body distinct from his soul is to be expunged; this I shall do, by printing in the infernal method, by corrosives, which in Hell are salutary and medicinal, melting apparent surfaces away, and displaying the infinite which was hid.

— William Blake, *The Marriage of Heaven and Hell*

O Rose thou art sick.

— William Blake, "The Sick Rose"

The unseen sun is raying into a street
of cloud and rain, and spotlighting small gusts,
openings of soft, burning-clear spring air
wheeling out through the cloud, and quick ghost rain,
glassy, vapour-hazed, flying into them
and disappearing in brightening light,
a street no longer a street but Blake's tray,
and in it an immersed plate.
The turnings
of the acids are the soul arriving
from above to embrace and kiss the lips
of the body waiting kneeling with arms
uplifted in unfettered ecstasy
on the grave, each waking and wakened by
the other, each displaying the hidden,
never hidden infinite in each other
to each other at last.
The workshop mist
subsides, the air's radiant travelling
fury turns to calm, the eye melts away
with everything it has held, then the day
reappears as a bush in full flower,
and there, and again there, is the healed rose
of the body and soul's reunion,
subtle, minute, immaculate, still drops
dotting its sleepless petals.

The new plate
executed, it will print its image
of what those who go to find love will find
in the depths of the body, and not know
they end division of heaven and hell,
two birds that will alight on a rose-bush
to sing their uncanny joy, and not know
whether they are birds or mirroring rain.

II

NIGHT NEAR TRIKALA

Back from an anonymous roadside village
where I had sat outside beneath the brilliant skull of the moon
and eaten plate after plate of food with friends
and talked and drunk sharp Greek wine late into the night,
and not wanted ever to live in any time other than that night
and not wanted ever to be anywhere other than there,
where the conversation had cornered me and invited me
to be exactly everything of who and what I was,
and to know a single and unending instant
of an intoxication of fury and delight
in which both logic and intuition flowed through me like wine,
I arrived at the hotel I stayed at in a small city
and found it locked for the night, and my door key lost,
and I slept on a bench in the central square,
feeling as if I had drunk of the earth,
face to the voluptuous, cool, grape-dark sky,
and the new stars with their millions-of-years-old light
that spread over me like glittering keys, like new senses,
and imagining I might never wake again,
or ever open the same eyes again, for they would go
making their own way in amongst people, in amongst gods.

Larissa

THESSALONIKI TRAIN STATION

We were on the train, waiting for it to depart
and leaning out the window.
"Are you English?" he shouted at me. "I speak English.
Thank you. It's a nice day.
Are you Yugoslav? I speak Serbo-Croatian.
Are you German? I speak German."
And so it went, on and on, it seemed he knew
at least a few words of ten or twenty languages.
"Are you French? I speak French.
Are you Turkish? I speak Turkish."
He was grinning, his face sweating and glistening,
standing as if at attention, talking non-stop to his audience,
surrounded by old suitcases, cardboard boxes, and paper bags
all spilling out the array of his belongings,
clothes, books, even small appliances,
and continually hitching up his woeful pants
that kept trying to fall down.
There were people from so many places on the train,
African students, Soviets of Greek descent
arriving in Greece for the first time, carrying caches
of hair combs to sell in the bazaars,
righteous young Brits and Americans with backpacks,
Dutch tourists, German tourists, Swedish tourists,
melancholy old Greek women, Greek families, Greek Gypsies,
and nervous, exhausted Albanians on the run —
all had their ideas about who and what the man was.
Many claimed they had heard of him —
he had just gotten out of jail,
he had been a Greek government official and swindler,
he was a wealthy businessman on an alcoholic adventure,
he was a renowned gambler who had lost everything.
Everyone seemed to feel they knew him —
some even claimed he was a stand-up comic gone awry,
others recalled him as an ex-sitcom star.

"Are you Italian? I speak Italian.
Are you Danish? I speak Danish."
He was the different parts of whatever he called himself
flying out in a hundred directions,
he was a wildly flashing switchboard,
he was the king bagman of the world,
living in train stations, on trains and train platforms
and sputtering out language after language,
he was the living ramshackle spirit of the tower of Babel
calling out to all the train passengers in the world
as to workers who could no longer understand one another
and were dispersing to come back and complete the labour
or the great tower would stay unfinished forever,
calling out to all who to him seemed confused
though they also seemed certain where they were going.

THE CHURCHES OF SKOPELOS

Waking suddenly in the island room,
the balcony curtain blowing aside
and flaring as if ablaze in the sun,
I heard a woman singing unaccompanied,
her voice so clear, the melody so strange,
so familiar, it was painful to me,
in her voice every joy and sorrow
was signed up somewhere in clear flowing flame,
and I thought it had to be a dream, for
I felt the singing inside my body,
all my organs singing to each other,
but here I was wide awake.

And I knew
what I was hearing was emanating
from some not far off church. And so I roused
the woman who lay asleep beside me,
and we dressed and rushed outside, where I heard
other church singing, and rhythmic praying,
all crisscrossing in the crystalline air,
and beautiful and pure, but none of it
was the singing that had awakened me.
We were at the base of a small steep hill,
the church nearest us was at the hill's crest,
we walked to it and listened at its door,
but neither could I hear the singing here,
so now we began following a path
of our own making from church to filled church
in slow, wandering search of her.

We spent
the day in the lit hillside labyrinth
of winding streets, trying to find as many
of the two hundred churches in the town
of Skopelos as we could, some of them
in sidestreets like crannies, places only
the island's cats visited, some of them

almost anonymous in the hushed midst
of the blue and red house doors in cul-de-sacs,
some of them, cliff outcrops, radiant white
in the sun, like calm white birds in their nests.
At the last church we would come to, dozens
of people crowded around the entrance,
and they were all smiling softly, it was
as if we had found a celebration.
It was afternoon now, the sun pouring
down marble light, the shadows on the ground
black as black construction paper. We went
in where it was cool and evening-dark,
lit only by long thin hand-held candles,
and stood there in the small rough-hewn stone church
among those praying for the soul of a man
who had died a year earlier. The priest
was intoning from an aged large prayer
book open before him on its dark stand,
framed icons coated with gold, depictions
carved subtly in wood, and fathomless saints'
presences painted in primary colours
looked out at us from the whitewashed walls,
but no woman singer was here, nor, as
far as anyone we spoke to knew, had one
ever been here. I thought, nevertheless,
she must have sung her mysterious song
in the morning in a church like this one.
At the bright entrance they were handing out
pieces of honey cake, and they gave some
to the woman who had brought me to this place,
she touched my arm, gave me the cake in turn,
and I tasted its sweetness, happy, at home
in the gathering, one of the mourners.

HYDRA GREAT FRIDAY

We are out walking, and go into a church
and take candles in our hands and light them
and go back out and join the procession,
the hundreds of others with lit candles
winding slowly through the hushed labyrinth
of narrow stone streets, the waiting blackness
opening around each arriving flame
and each held-out hand, each candle of bone
carried in its own dark within the dark.
The holy bier, the gold-embroidered pall
covered with all the flowers of the spring
bunched or woven into wreaths, and sprinkled
with lemon leaves and rose petals, passed this way.
The women are still here who threw incense
on vessels of embers and made the air
smell sweet as the bier passed before their homes,
icons of Christ crucified and white plates
of green barley outside their open doors.
We are silent, and I simply follow
and lead in half-ignorant reverence
through dark like layers of beautiful soot
until we come to the sand of a small bay,
the procession now a large crowd gathered
where priests stand together in the water,
one swinging out incense towards the shore,
another reciting from a prayer book
a passage about repentance and death,
the words floating heavily back and forth,
back and forth across the air on the sea.
One steadies an effigy of Judas
tied to a pole, and when he sets it on fire,
bright reflections loosen over the waves
and light up the faces of old women
closest to the water, faces of waiting.

I stand at the back of the crowd and think
of no betrayer or man nailed to a cross,
but of how the beloved when they are gone
become the exact limits of those alive,
and edge the living loneliness, of how
the dead have died to send the sorrowing
out to their lives as to a procession
which will take them with others through a dark
limitless and still a perfect prayer-niche
for any candle, for the eyes of any
making their way in a lit frame of bones
through all the holy dead to the first birth.

OUZO

You add water to a glass of ouzo
and a genie-less smoke rises in it asking: What is it you wish?
the ardent clear spirit distilled from the lees of wine
suddenly wreathed in opalescent fumes,
and boiling away the sediment of your life, and distilling the day
while you sit at a rough table in the mid-morning in front of the sea —
so you see in the glass the vaporous myth of Plato's cave,
the man bound in chains, the theatre of shadows,
and beyond this, the sun's world-filling light,
and the day becomes simpler and simpler;
the day wakes you into light, and you drink thick coffee,
walk and swim and sleep in the afternoon,
and sit and wait for the blackness of the night to bloom
and the small brilliant white multitudinous flowers of the stars
to bloom from infinitely within the night's blooming.
And there is nothing here to wish for except what is —
nothing except the instant opening,
the sea clear as alcohol, the collapsed waves' foam bubbles
crackling along the sand like a delicate fire,
the distinct self-scoured sand grains, glasses of ouzo themselves,
and the nearby profusion of houses, all exquisite white words
strung around the hills, and the hills a smile of death.
And the old waiter who sets down the ouzo,
who makes his way without effort and with a strange beauty
around and around the perfectly arranged tables —
I see now he is the man who broke free of his chains
and walked out of the cave into the light of day,
and it is as if he is the first person I have ever seen,
and I do not know how it is that the wrinkles of his face
seem to multiply in the sun, nor how I now look at him through eyes
that are not mine, and he only smiles, for they are his eyes,
nor how it is that he is also young;
now his eyes ask me what it is I wish, and he already knows

that it can be nothing except to wait for all blackness to deepen
and become one with all light, and the hills here as they darken
and the sun's fire, come into clarity,
to wait for the world to re-collect the world,
and every question I have ever asked to return to me
and place me in the chains of metaphor, in the absolute
made of the chains' flowing, of what is transparent.

Skopelos

THE MONASTERIES OF THE AIR

At the summits of isolated craggy pillars —
the remains of eroded mountains
that stood at the edge of the Greek plain —
sit hundreds-of-years-old stone structures
like an uncanny unmoving gathering.
                                        We walk up
almost vertical interminable stairs
to the principal, still lived-in monastery, once
accessible only by rope and net.
                                        Here, a thousand feet
above tilled ground, the sun lets light
fall with great purity into scrupulous gardens,
doorways, clean stone paths.
                              I follow others
into a museum displaying monks' icon work,
the code faces of saints and virgin and child,
and different medieval tools, and all the apparatuses
for hauling things up from below. The entire area,
we are told, was devastated during the last war,
but the monastery could not be touched,
and every monk took part in the resistance,
feeding people, hiding people.
                                    I enter a monk's cell,
a small cave, a stone nest for a man.
There is a cistern, there is a rough shelf in the rock.
How many fasted and prayed here, I wonder.
How many, in peacetime and in wartime,
fought to die before they died?
                                        There is a window
in the rock, and I lean my head out, look down,
and see the Thessalian villages sparkling,
and the fields of fruit and vegetables and cotton,
all seemingly spinning slowly. It is when
I turn, and face the cell interior again,
that I hear what I heard within the quiet

the first moment I stood here
without telling myself I heard it.
                                        What was it
that long sustained the solitary aspirant
if not this air, this ceaseless, breathy, hypnotic flow —
the cell is perched in it and contains it.
What was it that the aspirant learned
if not that he had to be a worshipper
of the measureless current, and pray to the praying air.
What was it that the texts had tried to teach him
if not the unteachable secret in this air.
Here in his high poor cell, encased by rock,
encased by his body, with this air inside,
while the window blazed light, and blazed darkness,
and blazed light again, hearing the air, he had
his more-than-definition of God, and his more-than-proof.

Meteora

ORISTE

In every market and shop and taverna
they are saying "*Oriste! Oriste!*"
meaning "May I help you?" or "At your service"
but not so nice or courteous-sounding;

literally, "I'm listening,"
and when translated into English
for the benefit of non-Greeks,
"What do you want?"

More assertion than question,
a word without wavering in it,
without pretense, without false graces,
like a perfect form,
like a marble column,
the sheer lines cutting the light.

Not a plea, and not a prayer,
and still, a word like an act
of clear, hard love
for the god who is everywhere and does not exist,
who cannot be described or conceived of,
who is revealed in every stranger who walks in.
"*Oriste*!" What do you want? I'm listening.

Larissa

LARISSA BAPTISM

The child being baptized, not an infant but aged eight or ten,
had been born to a Greek father and a Japanese mother,
and because the father's family was well known in the town
the child was surrounded by a large crowd of people
that pressed close, curious to see the naked, shivering, and shrieking
half-Oriental girl put into a metal tub full of water.
The priest, his tone unvarying, was reciting the ministrant words,
all the time swinging an incense-container back and forth on its chain,
sending out disappearing streams of scented smoke-mist.

The moist fumes and the echoey huge-domed church air
suddenly turned cold, the cold of the air after a winter rain.
And it seemed to me I stood at a cold, thick-rushing creek
in a half-hidden ravine half a world away from this place —
the grid of the suburban streets above had been vanquished by fog,
and beside me, the fog travelling down through the ravine
had wound together all the trunks of the creekside trees.
And swirling and rippling around the random creek bed rock, the creek
    water
was a white lustrous ore melting and running toward me.

The people, chattering, and coiffed and arrayed as for a television
    camera,
and the bored-looking priest, were moving their mouths but were
    silent.
The child's crying was a wire of sound beyond hearing
that ran up through the base of my brain, taut with strange terror.
Now the child would be received into the congregation —
I knew I would find, and not find, another, elsewhere.
I heard myself ask myself in my heart: Am I a child
or an old man? What am I that all I want to do is pray ceaselessly
to what I cannot know, to what may or may not know me?

LEMON GROVES

The horizon a burnt-out eye socket,
the sea a throng of mouths wounding themselves against sand —
the only shelter was inside the car,
so we drove down the peninsula just to drive,
until we came to a tract of green trees
running inland from the road and to the land's end.
We parked and went in amongst lemon groves,
vast flowering lemon groves, releasing fragrance for miles.
And we walked together then as if we had both
come under the spell of the scent, as if nothing
could be so apparent and destined as this: that within the scent
the trees' white flowers sent out lay the leaf-shaded rinds
of the ripe lemons, the small pert yellow spheres;
that within the fruit, within the sudden dream, at the end
of our journey through the bewildering black glare
of the sun, shone the light of the lemon,
and we stood finally in its bliss-shedding ray.
There, clasped beyond burning sight, we dwelt in each other
as in a single cool sanctuary
where whatever we knew of bitterness and hurt
became the pure decision in us, nourishing and healing,
the secret, in the midst of burning change,
which would make us clear, clean-edged, purged of doubt.

Nafplion

EPIDAUROS

Here, by chance, I heard Cavafy's *Ithaca* recited
with the sun going down in the olive, orange, and lemon groves
that cover all the hills of the undulating horizon,
the sky itself filled with orange and yellow hues,
insubstantial chasms in the air of burning grief and rapture,
the sounds of the Greek words arranging themselves in the air.
Ithaca gave you the marvellous journey.
Without her you wouldn't have set out.
She has nothing left to give you now.
And if you find her poor, Ithaca won't have fooled you.
Wise as you will have become, so full of experience,
You'll have understood by then
What these Ithacas mean.
And then silence, pure crystal silence,
and stillness, sudden healing stillness,
through which the body may be made one with the spirit,
the sound unheard, the soul of all sound,
an Ithaca of silence, silence made manifest
through the sacred geometry of the theatre stone,
a Lady of Silence, of the secret of secrets,
energy unbound, which has brought forth every poem,
every grief and union,
and contains every as yet unwritten poem,
bodiless and radiant, as she is,
waiting to enter into the circle of recited sound
and contain in itself stillness and silence.

III

THE CURTAIN

Why a little curtain of flesh on the bed of our desire?
— William Blake, *The Book of Thel*

. . .the blurred touch through the curtain.
— W.B. Yeats, the *Letters*

In the soundless travelling dazzle
of the afternoon sunlight

after the rain and mist have disappeared,
at a turn in the creek where it has come to run level,

the quickly swaying water
is the movement of your waist.

In its cold longing, the water is uncovering you,
drawing a curtain aside,

and drawing another over you
in a deepening clarity —

the way my hands, as you let the blurred touch
interpret the light, and veil you

in the dreaming of the flesh,
find a caress.

So you may become bright, you become dark again,
darker than before.

The creek turns, and flows through itself,
and frees the loss beyond loss

of the water's pure searching,
hides, and binds it.

THE MIST

Mist is rolling like a flood down the sky,
down through the canyon, between the high dark walls of the trees,
slow lightning in it, the rush of new metal,
furious, serene cloud-fumes the stars almost fall into;
it follows the river like another river, always leaves itself, as the river does;
it is radiant in its ghostly surprise,
in its certainty, in its endless question.
It touches two human faces,
faces of ones suddenly both old and infant-like —
the mist-particles are their mirror; the mirror returns their gazes;
the two stand side by side gazing like mist.
The river
shatters at their feet, from its end to its beginning;
its white calligraphy writes, erases itself;
the river is a wild, translucent marrow —
in the bright, dark dazzle of the river spray,
in the thickening flow of the mist, the two disappear.
Now they will say,
and now the river will say, they are in heaven,
in heaven or in the depths of marrow,
in the depths of an unknown metal, in the depths of a mirror —
where nothing has begun to rot, within everything that rots;
now they will say, mist followed the river, found them,
drew them through its awe, made them one,
and made that oneness vanish before it itself vanished, before
it fell into a mirror, into the interior of a skeleton, into mist.

NORVAN PASS TRAIL

Rough route. Up past a strong waterfall
and off into a hushed rise, soft underfoot, guarded by trees,
never more than half-lit; then trickier terrain
of soaked bush, rock-faces, exposed roots,
light coming in erratic, sharp;
down into a chute, over rocks the mountain rolls down;
up again, the trail a twisting tunnel,
and small openings, sunlit air, crystal rain —
floating cold blank particulars.
                                        Multiple struck
cymbal notes of creeks everywhere
as you continue, creeks crashing unseen
through the trees and remaining in the trees as the trees,
and mountain-side mist, secret and visible,
the still silent music of creek origins in it;
then a high ledge alongside treetops; suddenly
you are out at deafening concentrated waters,
a creek with such rushing force it tilts you,
and will yank you away if you take
the smallest misstep, and thick mist
flowing wildly with it down a swerving gorge —
the filled unfathomable gorge of the body,
the single, first and last particular.
                                        Cold spirit
not at home anywhere visits here.
You can only skirt its edges, careful, frightened.
Whatever you think, it contains it, erases it.
You think you see it, but your eyes are only part of its eye
which you cannot even say is an eye,
and looks through you to an elsewhere
now travelling through you, directionless.
You feel as if that eye is on you,
and searches you, and recognizes you,
but if it does, it sees nothing you know.

RAVINE BURRS

I go up a ravine trail filled in with new bush,
heavily lying weeds, tall fountaining ferns,
many-tongued, wild flowering shrubbery,
overhanging tree branches weighted with plump leaves,
and sunlight seeming slowed down, wet and green,
all flowing over me while I try to trace hidden
but everywhere-boulder-parted-, bright-sounding
descending creek waters back towards their high source.
And at almost every step, burrs catch and cling
to my pants, shirt, and hair, until they cover me.
I could be telling the way up the ravine
by these waiting burrs, these pointed flower heads,
as when I have seen my way by a dream
I remember suddenly in the light of day.
It is spring, and, dark and untouched all winter,
the ravine now touches what comes to touch it;
so it is it lets burrs cover me and lead me
to where I approach the light at the top,
light sifting itself, turning clear now, fine and sharp.
It is the night I was led up a steep ravine trail
by three silent women, identical
and yet each more strangely exquisite in turn;
in the morning we arrived at lit open air
where a stream ran down a ledge before us
like a clear brilliant string thrown down out of the sky;
I stepped up abreast of the three women,
and somehow I was back near the creek mouth
in the dark mirror-light of a creekside cave;
there, a fourth woman who was all the other three
and none of them, beyond them, waited for me.

And now I come out into the light of a street;
the one in me that can never call the ravine home
stands in his burrs as in a prickly trap;
the one in me that will always call the ravine home
stands in the burrs as in the map of himself
the ravine gives him, the chart that shows him
the trail through centres, ushering into centres
the waters and dreams that flow through them and make him,
these dark-rayed stars, these constellations of the earth.

RAVINE MORNING

. . . where ever beauty appears
If in the morning sun I find it; there my eyes are fix'd
In happy copulation . . .

— William Blake, *Visions of the Daughters of Albion*

It is still half-dark out; darker in the ravine,
the dim light just shining down the night mist;
but within the mist, other light, the creekwater
surging with the night's rain, lightning flowing,
a single bolt old and new as the beginning;
it spasms forth ceaselessly through creek froth
into the creek as into its sanctuary and joy;
the first lightning strikes, and finds the world
and the world climbs back up through the lightning,
and the ravine fills with morning; the creek
turns the lightning-flash-white of living bone;
the lightning meets itself, strikes and flows back,
still striking; becomes two discovering
one another's beauty, and each creating
and becoming the other in a recurrent
quickly vanishing ecstasy; the creek-rush
and creek-way find one another, and find
what finds, and brighten together, the morning's clue
to the morning of mornings, and the mystery the eye
will follow and follow, lover and beloved.

CREEK TROUT

Silver, dark-spotted, each spot with a pale halo,
its sides striped with a rainbow band,

it is a flawless swimmer, and knows its way perfectly
through the water, as if its smooth, quick body

could feel the length of the creek,
from the mountain-side source of heavy rain to the inlet-meeting mouth.

To see the trout, to gaze after it
as the doors of the water open before it,

as the innumerable chambers of the creek open before it,
each chamber flowing through the other,

each a new exultation, a new feeling of the touch of the creek,
a new entering and entering,

is to look through water
in which the trout becomes a single brilliant journeying grain,

a darting purplish ray, a piece of the voluptuous refuse of the first stars,
a glimpse of a crystal look,

and it is to look through the trout
as through a living lens, imagining what the trout knows —

through flesh wholly a vivid eye,
blind sight seeing light before it shines —

before the trout as soon disappears
behind the final door of the water,

shimmering, shadowy traces, connecting up all its traces
somewhere on the other side of the world.

SPARROWS

for Florry

I. Morning

A handful of them,
their chirps the squeaks
of cloth after cloth
in quick succession
on the window —
then a pure silence,
then out of the nothing
so full it is peace,
they arrive again,
little emissaries
of what is looking
through the world
into the world,
now a deep-flushed
and wet-bright fruit,
a sudden cluster
of smiles in my ears.

II. Evening

Bits of grass
in their tiny beaks,
they are building
their nest in a cleft
in the dark blue
canyon rock of clouds;
the waiting air
is a microphone
for their voices,
and they create
the thunder, the rain,
and sit so lightly,
safe in the storm,
each all pulsating heart,
eyes black sparks
that become the night,
without thought,
without theory,
each the secret
no one knows.

WHERE WATER MEETS WATER

The secretive murmur and the recurring small splash
have brought me to a ditch-wide tributary of the creek —
I step through its vault of opulent bush
and into shadow and tricklings, gulpings, quick
drummings of birds' wings, foliage-muffled whistlings.
The tunnel that feeds the creek is far off,
so the water's path here is not man-made, it is a way
that the rain braiding together created on its own
at the end of its tumble down the mountain.
                                                                        I notice
how quiet it is, as if a door has shut
on the creek's clatter. It could be evening, it is half dark,
but it is the gloom of the green, and elsewhere
it is the middle of the summer day.
                                                            The way narrows
and swerves, and there in front of me, sunlight
falling freely through an opening overhead
as through a roofless church, is a calm brilliance, a shining.
It is an inch or so of the clearest water
treading long, lying down, wavering green grass,
it is other water that has made its way here
to lose itself in the tributary.
                                                    Yet where this water
meets water, it is a sifting lens, and this lens
collects me, it ushers and gathers me
into a new attention and hiddenness,
as if I were unborn, as if it were the foetus I was,
and now an egg of light and water, floating there
so still, translucent, able to resist the flow.

THE SEEDS OF THE FERN

If he were ever to touch the subtle heart
of the woman he loved, he would have to be a gatherer of the seeds of
the fern,
he would have to go in silence on Midsummer's Eve
between the hours of eleven and midnight to a chosen place
and lay a pewter dish under a forest fern
and bend the fern over with a forked hazel rod
and allow the seeds to fall.

Then if the seeker wore three of the seeds in his shoe
he would be made invisible, and if he ate the seeds
he would be given magical summoning power
over any creature that walked, flew, or swam —

for the seeds would take the seeker in his dream
into the silent seed, which folded within itself multitudes of ferns,
and the foliage each fern's frond held out
arranged in rows of other minute whole ferns, like a code,
and into the death out of which the seed had fallen,
the life into which the seed had dropped,
the death the seed would embrace again,
and finally, for an instant, into the most secret fern,
where the man would stand in himself as in a lit clearing
and see the sought-after woman at the clearing's edge
and know she had been there all along
and, as she stepped into the clearing,
feel her movements flow through him, clarity upon clarity, world upon
world.

RAVINE SEAGULL

A seagull overhead, gliding in and up —
it claps its wings against its flanks,
it lets out its cry, its searching touch
immediately finding the ravine from end to end
and making the creek water glitter
more brightly than before and darken
with more exquisite gloom, the trees
lift as out of a cold lament. The seagull's eye
might now be the instantaneous
single clear drop of an eye it is flying
through and opening and opening —
the eye of the ravine's beauty, in which the creek
is a flowing couch inlaid with the worked
brilliant ivory of the water's whitenesses
and adorned with lapis lazuli where the sky
falls free past the tree tops. The seagull's cry
might be for more sight, it might be made
of the joy of lovers that have lain down together
on the every-instant-newly-made
couch of their union. The seagull
has to keep flying up the ravine to keep
the thick sap lifting in the trees, to keep
the bower of the ravine luxuriant,
and the lovers turning as the creek waters turn.
If the seagull has ever flown in any air
other than here, or ever dreamt
of an eye creating an eye deep
within an eye, it does not know it. Still the gull
tears away a veil. Who can the two walking here
have ever been if not the two lying down
on the couch within the flowing drop,
and each the other's couch and flowing sight?

What can they do but return and return here
as to eyes rinsed and prepared for love,
though love may still be pure loss? The cry
they will hear will be their own seagull-singing
in love beyond their love. The creek water
will be the steady rush of the flesh they entwine,
letting them go through it, and by its light.

INTER-RIVER TRAIL

Between the two rushing down parallel rivers,
tall tree trunks standing in a winding row
are frames for the river mist blowing in and forming pictures —
quick drift-edged vapour metal, ghostly bright swirlings —
new mist continually arriving,
mist-panes filling with mist-codes of endless variation,
as if the rivers signalled their flow and ripple changes
up into the high forest between them,
and the signals met, and switched back and forth,
mist reflecting mist within moving mist.

Every movement that can ever be seen
in any window forms and re-forms in the mist,
every instant's pane a picture of the rivers' destinies,
every picture describing every other picture —
in the blowing mist-windows, the rivers' wind-eyes
filled as with indecipherable codes of creation,
charts of changes, future-revealing cards,
each card turning into another card,
each card a window on another card,
each a set of signals to another.

They hold up mist-cards from their flowing decks,
but the first and last, full card without content —
the chart of pure change, the changeless window
of unending empty glass, the blank card of origin —
the rivers never hold up, though the tree trunk frames
wait and wait to be clear of mist. And you between
the rivers, looking at card after card, you after you,
each describing you, the you that is the other,
and never appears. And you a river yourself,
and the pictures of what you do not know of the river.

BRIGHT SHOOTS OF EVERLASTINGNESS

But felt through all this fleshly dress
Bright shoots of everlastingness

— Henry Vaughan, "The Retreat"

The branch of a ravine maple tree
growing and slowly floating out and lengthening over the creek
is letting its leaves be houses for the light.

And for an instant
it is passing a leaf across my brow, no wind anywhere,
in a gesture that is familiar, as if I have reached out
and gestured to myself from the branch, the tree's green touch,
its blind sight —
it is trying to see me through its leaves, succeeding,
looking at me the way a night's dream
reaches out to me from within me.

And it has let a dream find itself —
a dream in which I followed a quick-moving old man,
and watched as he bounded up stairs to the side entrance of an
old house
where he entered an upper room,
a room like the green cell of a floating leaf.

Somehow I was there,
and saw the cold energy flowing through him, the cold brilliance in
his eyes,
as he sat at a desk and worked with a spread-out green material,
weaving small mirrors into it with long green threads issuing from
his hands,
bright shoots of everlastingness.

THE CLOAK

Where the creek ends at a tunnel you turn around
and begin the walk back up the ravine,
the creek rushing down as through a spinning out and weaving —
boulders and tree parts, spinning wheels and looms,
water an always materializing see-through cloth —
you make your way as in the midst of the water,
and it seems to admit you, and interlace you
into its glooms and brilliancies, its trembling clarities,
and slip a cloak around you, a manifold cloak
with an embroidery of secret signs where spirit rushes through,
and joy and sorrow cross, and are indistinguishable and still:
the creek, too, arrives at where the ravine ends and returns
instantaneously, doubling back through itself,
putting on its cloak which is nothing but itself,
the way a very old man sees more and more clearly
the face of the child he was in his own face, until the unfathomable soul
suddenly looks back at him out of his wrinkles,
the way lovers create a caress and rush through it
into what has never existed for them until then, rushing back
through themselves towards where they have always been,
the caress weaving and unweaving what they know.

THE WAKE

Art thou not it that hath cut Rahab, and wounded the dragon?
— Isaiah 51:9

He maketh a path to shine after him . . .
— Job 41:32

Drifting ships
echo in fog the wounds of Leviathan . . .
— Patrick Lane, "Stigmata"

The familiar foreign ships, those spaced along the inlet,
sound their fog horns; the repeating low notes
drag me asleep, and I swerve off the steep shore
and enter the always close waters —
where I awake again outside my room
creeping down a hallway oozing boiling ointment
closer to the door of the sea dragon's face;
I stand gazing at myself gazing at the fire
leaping out of the mouth of the unseen,
the voices, the man-snarls, the woman-shrieks,
dancing before an immense blazing liquid eye,
power and strangeness moving through it,
and my own glimpsed eye lost.
But I am the slayer
of the sea dragon, of the waters of chaos,
and take a carving knife to my arm
and teach the flesh to trust the blade —
and then run outside, where the still air watches me,
and the dark, glistening suburban lawns
ridicule me, for although my feet can almost make me fly,
it is because I am a ghost, and weightless,
because at each shut house gate I feel iron anguish,
and at each shut house door I am a known beggar.
There is a last door that opens — then such brightness
I cannot look up: a man and woman usher me
to a bathroom cabinet, to a den, to a plush chair.
When I open my eyes again it is in a head

propped between policemen. My father, unaware of us,
is stamping circles in his front yard.
And I am led away.
                                                  The morning's eyelid of light
will open; the brooding turning mountain,
the grave firs with their heavy, slowly gesturing boughs,
the travelling drizzle, the twisting, fluted creek —
it will all be the shining wake
of Leviathan whipping away from the field of vision;
I will be the trailing far end of the wake,
and yet I will be ahead of it, treading the ground
as if riding the wings of the wind; the ships
will still be out there, lying at anchor in the inlet,
made with the beams of my house laid in the waters,
their voices healing my wounds, and heralding them, human.

MORNING ON WICKANINNISH BEACH

Nothing of the ocean is visible
except the long shore-reaching wave
unrolling itself as if on a taut wire.
I walk along the tide line
inside the ocean's vast pearl-radiant mist fumes,
its visible musk, all tingling atoms
of fine-spun cloud-metal and brine.
The harsh heat
of the sun is held and undone, the glare is sifted,
the mist lets fall angel and marrow light on the wave,
the shore softness is a voluptuous coldness, a vast drop of dew
face close-up, a vast, infinitely subtle kiss.
I imagine
what is out there in the fierce, beautiful din —
the wheeling whitenesses of waves, the manifold forms
floating out of the waves into the air.
Yet the threshold
of the mist hides this. The shore-reaching wave
re-invents itself, arriving incandescent and gazing,
an eye that has discovered sleep and is now waking —
it is teaching me how to die.
The light-carrying
vessel of the wave crest smashes itself
on the morning of the world. The inch-deep
tidewater slides in, clear tablecloths
thrown out over the sand, the feast, the guests unseen,
clear loose sheets, sudden composition, unbound book pages
with all words written on them, all contained there
in a single secret transparent word.

Pacific Rim National Park,
Vancouver Island

SAVARY ISLAND LIGHT

Whole huge-limbed trees, sawn stumps
with worn upended roots the sea
has turned and turned in its hands,
errant logs the sea has stripped
and smoothed, and unrecognizable
sun-whitened shapes that hold
the lost curves the sea has made,
the miles-long untouched driftwood
is a wild structure like flame —
flame at rest, the wood's atoms
vibrating at a great speed,
so the wood is burning visibly
and is a fire along the beach,
pausing, still and watching itself.

We set up rough camp on the sand
and all day go to and from it
as a shelter in an hourglass
of the air and glistening hot light
in which each incoming
and withdrawing flame-like wave
pours the sea into the sea,
and the driftwood, one instant,
is the skeletal remains
of all the creatures of the earth
that have ever lived, manifold
interconnected houses of bone
now vacant, the next instant,
house walls and a house-gutting fire.

Whatever we can know of love,
it is here when we look at anything,
and disappears here as in a fire
that saw itself a first and last time
before it began travelling
in the sea-labyrinth of blindness

of the creation it became
in the first split-instant,
and the light looks back at us now
as if we were its prophecy,
as if the pupil of an eye
held its secret it did not know
until it gazed, like a person,
into a mirror for the first time.

Before we were each who we are,
we were here, we were like light
in the first, ongoing instant
when the light hid itself
in houses that had to catch fire,
and love became a loneliness
within the houses' blackened walls —
we saw the driftwood flame
of the light, the air, the hourglass
of sight pouring the world
into the world, we knew the light
as if it were the lost person
of persons, as if it were light
forever travelling to light.

Savary Island,
south shore

A MEMORY OF A DEER

It had come down into the city
out of the mountains in the night
and gotten lost, had sensed the dawn,
heard car noises at the corner,
heard the police station and hospital
across the street, and, bewildered,
come into this silence and deeper dark
within the still-dark morning to hide.
Now I, a human, had approached it.
And the deer stood there like a child
caught doing something wrong.

Once I was told that years ago
in summer, deer would come down
out of the humming mountains
through the night and keep going,
swimming the mile-wide inlet
from North Van to downtown.
The city wharves would stop them,
and they would struggle for hours,
trying and trying to get ashore.
In the morning, men would drag up
the exhausted or dead deer
like fish into the nets of their arms.

And once, desperate and dazed, I entered
those cold dark waters, held on
to a broken old wharf that sat there
near the foot of Lonsdale Avenue,
then pushed myself into the inlet
with the intention of swimming out
farther than I could swim back.
But came back, with no idea why,
with no need to know why,
only my own weeping and laughing.

It must have been the memory
of that underground parking lot deer
already coming to life in me
that took me down to the water
that night and made me swim out
and also made me turn around.
Then, the memory must have been
just a pinpoint hidden in my body,
but a light which would begin to burn
and lead me without my knowing it
through time to another night
and to where the deer stood in the dark —
so the light could become the deer,
and the deer, a vision of the deer:
its strong delicate-looking head
and neck as it swims across the water,
its forelegs, flexed haunches, and hind legs
as it lifts itself onto a wharf,
and begins its run through the city
to a forest and a secret herd.

IV

LAZARUS' SONGS TO MARY MAGDALENE

I.

When Jesus saw her weeping . . . he groaned in the spirit,
and was troubled.

— John 11:33

I had left life behind, but even so,
when he called I could hear his sudden longing,
and I knew it was the fierce clear brightness
of his longing I felt rise like dawn through my blood.

His voice hurt me, his calling me to come out,
to take breath again, commanded the same sickness
that had ruined me to fill me again,
and it was as if coming back were another death.

The common shroud I had been buried in
had come unwound, revealing my bandages —
they were filthy, and hung off me like rags.

I was covered in open wounds, but these
wounds were my eyes, and through them, light saw you,
arraying you in every story of love.

II.

It was Mary which anointed the Lord with
ointment. . . whose brother Lazarus was sick.

—John 11:2

When you knelt before him, and washed his feet
with your tears, and dried them with the hair of your head,
and anointed him with precious ointment,
that was when my own destiny began.

Your hands on him, and your worshipful lips
kissing his feet, were a slow and desperate
prayer of love beneath all silences.
I knew he would love you like no other.

When he said to his disciples to take
the stone away from the grave in which I had lain
dead and rotting for four days, he did so

because he could no longer withhold his love for you,
and because to him the world had become a door
through which he sought the world and found himself.

III.

Jesus saith unto her, Woman, why weepest thou?
Whom seekest thou?

— John 20:15

If you ask what it was like, I will tell you:
I knew I had no eyes with which to see,
no ears with which to hear, and knew nothing
else, not anything of whom I had been

in life, and not any feeling at all
until he called. It is only now, having come back,
that I have a vision of a man and woman —
they are embracing with infinite care,

and now they are shattering in each other's arms,
and the pieces of them are the fragments
of a shattering brilliant mirror.

Each piece seems to be crying out "I love you"
but the man and woman have disappeared,
and the words are the dazzling, soundless light.

IV.

And he that was dead came forth . . . Jesus saith unto them, Loose him, and let him go.

—John 11:44

When I took my first new, faltering steps
into the midday light, I stepped into his love.
I knew in the strangeness of my body
he had asked himself: Who is it I love?

And I knew he had sent his love down into rock,
tracing all the agony of his love
back down to its root, back down to deep rock
where there were no names, no him and no you.

I knew he had asked himself: How could I
have ever refused you? For his refusal
had been useless; the chains he felt imprisoned in,

and felt were somehow you, were his own flesh,
his own marrow. And if he let himself
become those chains, the chains would melt away.

V.

And there was a certain beggar named Lazarus,
which was laid at his gate, full of sores.

— Luke 16:20

It seems my body's wounds will never heal,
for they close only to open and bleed again —
it is they that are immortal in me.
The pain, too, I know will live forever.

Often I dream that invisible birds
are perched in the recesses of my wounds —
they come and go as if I sent them out
like the raven and the dove. Is the soul an ark?

When his soul learned touch, discovering the missing
parts of itself in your body, it came ashore
in his body and touched his deepest dream.

You effaced him then in the syllables
of his never having seen anything but you,
and slowly you named him as you are named.

VI.

. . . she hath washed my feet with tears, and wiped them with the hairs of her head.

— Luke 7:44

Your tears, your vivid tears, fall like your hair,
the long and sweeping down tresses of your hair —
always you are trying to catch your tears
with your upturned and waiting, bewildering

fingertips, and somehow hold your tears close,
and take them to yourself, as if they were children,
as if they were orphans, and they themselves
were weeping to be chosen, to have a home.

Like your tears, travelling and lost in you,
like your tears, trying to return to you,
he, too, was trying to find you, and he

would pray to his hands to invent themselves
so he might at last find the doves he knew
were crying beneath your skin and seeking his hands.

VII.

And he turned to the woman . . .

— Luke 7:44

Because he had left everything but you,
because he had shed everything he knew to shed
beside you, you showed him he had not yet begun.
He felt his blood, but it was not enough:

beyond his blood, beyond his hidden self,
he sang to you as a wave at its height,
the wild, locked-in, sourceless grief breaking free,
the bright foam erupting at the wave's tip —

a thousand saviours' cries of abandonment —
and this was the furious and beautiful
moment when he was one with you at last,

when neither of you were any longer who you
knew yourselves to be, when you had unclothed
yourselves of all beginnings, all endings.

VIII.

. . . Her sins, which are many, are forgiven; for
she loved much: but to whom little is forgiven,
the same loveth little.

— Luke 7:47

Because you love words, you made him summon
what was wordless and suffering in you
into the nakedness of his own eyes.
All his words, so gentle and powerful,

they did nothing if they did not call out
their claim on you, but could never claim you
any more than he could claim eyes, or claim the sight
that eyes find, when to see you was to know

it was you who looked out through his pupils' blackness.
For him you were the only one in whose
shining, searching eyes sorrow had concealed itself,

as if ashamed of its eternity,
so he might see your eyes as beautiful
if he prayed to words to let him see beyond them.

IX.

And the twelve were with him . . . and certain women . . .
Mary Magdalene, out of whom went seven devils . . .
— Luke 8:1-2

And when you finally lay with him nightly
and with your body burnished his body,
it was not unlike dying, and when you
made his body incandescent, and ignited it,

you who had brought your drunken heart to him,
you who had always been one who waited
as if water thirsted, as if new bread hungered,
you turned him into fire, and his soul rode the fire.

You extinguished him then in the harmless flames
that weave the world's scattered parts together,
you let him burn within that composure

that is your unutterable beauty,
that is the colourless eye of the world,
you let him feed it like inexhaustible oil.